BEING BEN

BENJAMIN LAMMEKI MAJAW

To my emotions,

for showing me love and patience.

To my passion,

for giving me a freedom to venture with my goals.

To my character,

for showing me perseverance.

To my youth,

for all the memories I love connecting again.

Contents

Preface vii

Part 1

1. We Were Just Kids 3

2. And Now We Have Grown Older 5

3. Courage Was A Part Of Me 8

4. And So Was A Passion For Love 11

Part 2

5. I Never Knew Books To Be My True Companions Now 15

6. And A Yearn For Connection With Different People 18

7. And Their Culture 21

8. My Love For Dogs 22

9. And A Passion For Portrait Arts 23

10. Oh! And Football 24

Final Words 31

Preface

During my youth, I had the thought to become a software engineer one day. It wasn't just a small thought. I took a pen and wrote it down on my dairy.

I got my first pen after my class 4 in school. And my dairy was filled with notes on anything I can keep as a memory. There were even notes from my friends before winter holidays started.

I was an avid learner in school.

Growing up, my passion and goals changed.

I had to venture a different path forward.

I was in a relationship after college. She was the most genuine person who, now I can understand, helped me connect with myself and nature.

Solitude.

I found the passion to read, connect with people, find love in the small things alone, writing, sketching, and sharing a close bond with my close friend from a Nyishi tribe.

She shares a thought, "Ben, you are a forever learner."

Yes, I am, Loge.

Payalincho.

Part 1

Growth and Downfall

CHAPTER I

We were just kids

I was so fond of her.
She was my classmate in class 5.
I did not know I had a crush or a feeling of affection for my friend.
We spoke very little with each other during that year - because we were always in our separate benches.

Knowing me as a kid, I always strive to work hard in studies. That year was when I knew even my classmates were hard working too. It was the first year we wrote our term exams with our pens.

I remembered the night before school started, I told my dad that we were supposed to be writing with pens from the next day, and gladly he gave me a ball point pen to carry with me.

Our classroom was in the second floor. And we had table lunches outside in the corridor to have our food. There was a total of four class rooms in that corridor. I remember during our singing classes we had to stand in a queue to get our notes checked by the teacher in charge. The interesting part was – if she found any spelling or punctuation mistakes, she would tell us to check again and again or even throw our notebooks in annoyance. But the intriguing part was – me and my friends would compete who would copy the song written by the teacher on the board faster. With that determination and keeping a keen eye for small carelessness, our singing classes were not at all boring.

I got a diary from my dad. Or should I say – I borrowed it from a storeroom and then told my dad about it. The notes I kept in my diary were written in pencil. I could recall my mum sharing her thoughts with my dad, on the notes I had written about my classmate. That was late in the evening while I was watching some cartoons with my brothers. The notes were my feelings of affection for that one girl in my class. The pages were filled with my neat handwritings. At least four pages if I could recall, were some thoughts about her.

We were very close in class 7. She taught me some notes in her language –

"Timrō nāma kē hō?

Timīlē khānā khāyau?

Kē timīlā'ī ma mana parcha?

Malā'ī timī dhērai mana parcha."

Seeing this in most schooldays, my classmates eventually teased me with my friend.

But we did not mind.

She would ask me for some mathematical calculations that she could not solve. I was obliged to help her always.

One day she showed me her childhood picture. She had the same smile since childhood. I also showed mine.

We had a songbook to ourselves. We wrote lyrics. It was just ours.

Knowing me as a 13-year-old, I kept my focus on books. Well, I do keep my dairy and that songbook. But the subjects we had were more of interest to me.

I remember, one morning I woke up at 5, for revision on the subject I was going to appear on that day.

That year was one of the best years I had as a student.

and now we have grown older

I saw the person whom I liked before again after class 10. She left school after class 8. We did not say our goodbyes before.

We then met online.

We have grown up now.

I do want to build a connection, or have a small conversation with her again.

We are not in the same state anymore.

I feel our bond has ended.

It was never a long and committed friendship – which I have always long for with her.

Class 7, I was in a committed friendship with a school boarder. We were really close and our friendship was really special. We would spend our time talking after school has ended. So, my days during class 7 were different.My school academic performance was underachieved. Maths was a trouble. And so was Health Education. I eventually picked up track before the final examination and got a 3rd position in class.

Since class 5, each year before winter, I would ask few of my friends to write something on a diary. They were 1 or 2 paragraphs of beautiful thoughts – with great meanings to me, and I would read them again and again.

Kamsen, who was my close friend, shared a thought about me and also encouraged me to do well in my 'egg-jumps' and the years ahead. She's brilliant.

The next year was the happiest of my schooldays.

As a student and as an individual.

As an individual, I was the most confident. But humility was part of me. And I learned to be humble always. Respectfully, the teachers saw that in me and throughout my years I feel appreciated in my work and speech. And that made me close to them.

As a student, I kept striving in my studies. Being top of class in all of the term examinations. It was hard work. But also, it was a passion for me to study.

Interesting, right?

Class 9 was when I hit rock bottom in my studies.

It was a huge and sudden downfall.

I felt I could not keep up with the tests or the subjects or the 80-marks-paper.

First term examination was excruciatingly embarrassing.

Results day came, the teachers explained that the drop in percentage was quite normal since class 9 was a different level compared to class 8. It was close to a state's level examination. My parents were surprised and sad. I soon was getting thrashes or scoldings by the teachers. They pushed me to study harder. To focus better. To give more time. An incident happened to me during class 9. And that brought my confidence to even a lower level. The friends I had were different acquaintances. They wasted my time in their nonsense.

There was a friend I had, and I was perplexed by what I have learned from him. Eventually, we were distant. Class 10 was a year to forget too. I was entrusted with the duties of a Head-Boy of the school. And I could not even do the smallest task confidently. I was overburdened by the constant pressure put on by my class teacher – which I completely respect her words now. There was not a place for me to rest my feelings or thoughts. All I could experience was the feeling of aloneness and lost.

On a positive note – my class 10 overall percentage was 83. **Surely, we did grow up fast.**

CHAPTER III

Courage was a part of me

As a student, I was really desperate for that same level of confidence I had when I was a kid back in class 8. Class 9 totally changed me. Class 10 made me so small of a person in my mind, that I would not want to revisit those feelings.
I needed therapy.
A breath of fresh air.
A long for peace and calmness.
Classes 11 and 12 tarnished my expectations of reaching high in studies.
I did meet some good friends during those years.
    I then got into college for my Bachelors.
It was never my decision.
All I wanted was **Fine Arts.**
To learn painting, and more, but I continued studying Science.
But I kept my focus during the first two years.
It was definitely a change of atmosphere. New friends and teachers.
The topics were interesting. **Integrals and Simple Harmonic Motion** were my favourite. The common thing between them: graphs

Samuel taught me a good amount of football.
He taught me how to control the ball, how to dribble and how to pass accurately.
We were really good friends. He always had that brotherly attitude towards me. But he was also the one who made me bunk those 7th period classes for football in a small

muddy field. We join alliances with Economics, Statistics and Geology department. And they too played with us. We even would arrange matches to be played in a golf course. So, college was filled with excitement, focus and football. These really brought my confidence up!

3rd Semester was the best time I did spend in college. Library, Integrals, Physics were surprisingly in tune with me. I could practice integrals anywhere. Lab, library, campus.

What was not in tune was programming.

The theory was about 70% but practical 30%.

And I was not confident until the end of my course.

But the most important memory I had from my college years, was the time I really gained confidence and how it boosted my productivity with Maths or even Physics.

COVID hid our state and our exams plus classes were online.

And I was not regular with the classes.

My beloved grand-dad passed away.

I soon went into depression mode.

I had no idea then.

Life whilst **only** at home changed me.

Before lockdown, I played football until 6PM in a turf ground.

Played with friends in college, go to the library, canteen, or just roam around.

I was never happy at home.

Most days I would sleep at late hours while watching the television.

Shows like "The Office", "Dexter" intrigued me.

On the year earlier, I kept a routine on Excel. I followed it well.

Online classes were present every day. I felt so bored.

I learned French.

Kept with the schedule daily.

Podcasts. That was my afternoon session with the language.

I soon began to develop a keen and optimistic interest in many languages.

I'm happy that French was my first love with languages. The accent is quite romantic in itself, I believe.

Vox. A channel I love back then on YouTube.

I still played outside my terrace in the morning. Working on improving my ball control.

Push-ups. I'd do 600 in a week.

And for about a month.

Meals were important.

"Who are you!?"

Loge went hysterical with my story:

It was in the evening. I had the idea of approaching girls to boost my confidence with them a little.

"Where is the coffee shop?", I asked her.

"Straight down", she answered.

A pause.

"Oh, hey, what's your name?", I asked.

She was perplexed. "Who are you!?"

A sense of curiosity.

CHAPTER IV

and so was a passion for love

The passing of my grand-dad did fill me with emotions of confusion.

I was terribly sad and lost.

I could not confide my feelings with anyone.

I soon kept my focus on college studies for a while and decided to prepare for CDS, which is an entrance exam for army aspirants. My preparation became a small passion. And I could feel a connection with it.

Until, I was hit with the news I had a back paper. Physics in 4th Semester.

It was my irresponsibility, my lack of focus, my self-doubt.

I told the head-of-department about my struggle with depression.

She could understand my feelings of need for someone, **like a kid who lost a best friend**.

She helped me figured some of the tasks I had to do.

My beautiful grandma from my father's side, passed away that same year.

Before I went to college, my dad got the news. He told me to come home early from college.

I was in going to appear for my 5th Semester exams in the coming weeks.

I wasn't ready. I wasn't motivated to do my exams. I became distant from the friends who were close to me. I wasn't close with the teachers either.

Clearly, my personality changed.

Exam month was done.
We started with the offline classes again.

Discipline was key to focus well in classes or at home.
I became irresponsible.

My attitude didn't change throughout the semester.
My final year ended.

I told dad that I won't be studying Computer Science anymore. He was appalled.

I told him I would be preparing for an entrance exam the following year. I had an interest for Mathematics.

I met my dearest Airisha Umdor online.
We were schoolmates in high-school.
Through her, I discovered love again.
Care, patience, integrity and trust. It bonded us together.
And we built a relationship together.
She was my beautiful woman.
A woman I cared the most because of the love we shared with one another.

My parents were unhappy.
It wasn't a surprise.

I had faith we'd overcome many challenges. We did.
We were terribly in love with each other.
We son had to break up.
I do terribly miss her.

Part 2

Solitude and Connections

CHAPTER V

I never knew books to be my true companions now

I fell in love with books at a very young age of 24.

We then built a connection.

A connection that will last forever.

I love carrying them on my backpack.

Anywhere I go.

Here's my story --

During my short stay in Tamil Nadu, I wanted to learn a few things on my own – reading, venturing alone, communicating, observing the surroundings. Reading became a habit because we had a small number of channels on the television. So, most of the time while resting, I would read. Tired of reading, I would venture alone. Oh! I was reading – **Think like a Monk by Jay Shetty.**

After my trip, I began to keep time for reading daily.

I would also highlight the lines I find interesting.

I soon had a passion to read.

It's something that I really wanted to do in the past.

I tried reading before too, but it never turned into a habit.

Although I love to research on different articles on the internet.

Researching on articles was interesting as well.

I've learned or studied alot from Vox channel, then I'd research more on the topic.

From climate change to the EU.

Well, anyways.

The Art of Being Alone - Renuka Gavrani

A milestone -
"The Art of being Alone" by Renuka Gavrani, was the first ever book I completed reading in 2024. It took me two months to finish the book after my trip. Because I do like to take the time to read and on different days. I slowly felt connected within a week of reading the book.

I soon began collecting books.

They say – when you love anything, you try to water it daily.

What I had to learn was patience.
Reading books taught me that.

I also love calmness more and a feeling of appreciating oneself.
I felt happy on the days I would venture alone on my cycle.
Or go to a calm place and just read.
That was my solitude.
My favourite time of the day.

One time I was just sleeping on some green meadow, looking at the clouds, the warmth of the sun was on my face. I could also feel the breeze, rushing.
Some children were playing.
The breeze would carry the ball in different directions and they would make a chase for it.
Joyful. Peace. Connections.

And I was reading.
It was a different connection.

It was my Ikigai.
My Ichigo Ichie.

Renuka Gavrani taught me solitude with loneliness. A connection with oneself.
She says – When you're alone, you are dealing with just one mind, one opinion and one perspective

"Being idle is a form of meditation

Have goals, personal goals, that is knowing yourself, what you can achieve.

Joy wouldn't come looking for you. It's you who has to find it, and if you cannot find it, then create the sources of joy in your life."

A line from Jay Shetty's 8 Rules of Love says –

"If a child grows up seeing love as protection, caretaking, loyalty, and sacrifice, that's what they identify as love."

Reading books illuminates me.

There's a feeling of joy.

Positivity.

I feel open to talk to anybody.

Jay Shetty says - **I had to be happy with myself**

And I had too also.

Finding solitude while being alone, reading books, connecting with different people.

That's my passion now.

My place of solitude has and will always be my connection with books...

and a yearn for connection with different people

After my relationship with my best friend ended, I was filled with emotions and questions.

Thoughts.

A feeling to talk to somebody about everything.

We did love each other a lot.

I just thought my parents could see that.

As time passed, I began to search for what I love. It might be anything small. Like a small lively walk or interaction with strangers.

They became a passion.

I made more companions.

From different states.

With different personalities.

I would love to listen and open up.

I had a different personality when I'm out.

A friend to anyone.

I carried on with this personality while meeting people on my trip to Tamil Nadu.

They would always love to see me greet them.

And I felt humbled to talk to them.

It was a small and kind connection.

They would then ask me questions – **Where am I from? Why are you here?**

I feel they always thought I was a lone foreigner.

A venturer.

A dream of mine is to connect with more people.

More languages to learn.

More stories to listen.

To look at different smiles.

To hold the hands of the old-aged and follow their steps.

That would have been a good entry for an ending.

But I do have more to say.

My great-granny.

She's a gem of a woman.

I do love to sit and listen to her during time of visits with my parents.

She passed away when I was in high school.

She would tell us stories from her past.

That made me want to connect with her more.

I had a habit of watching television in her house.

She would then call me to have some fruits.

Urging me to take from her basket.

Of course I'd feel happy to take some.

She'd asked me to sit by her bedside.

Then she'd start articulating her stories in her own pace.

She'd talk about the state of Meghalaya she saw before. Of course she's seen lots of intriguing change. She'd tell me about those old British cars operating. Ambassador cars.

She'd even share a tale how I was when I was a kid. I was truly close with her.

I am also really close with grandma now.

But sometimes it is just hard to find a good connection with her.

She makes it so easy to find some stories out of nowhere with me.

I'm happy to still find her in good health with the age that she has.

I'd definitely write a book about her too.

Here, in my state, there is a particular place where it's really diverse.

I do visit there often.

Venturing with my cycle.

I really love interacting with some of the people there.

A particular community called the Nagas, are a really humble community. It was through a friend I became part of their youth service church. I found a good connection with their youth pastor.

And as always, I became interested in that one girl. She was the lead singer of a praise and worship group. Spending time there gave me some new understanding about other tribes.

This is my passion.

To learn.

Because I am an avid learner.

CHAPTER VII

and their Culture

It is something so beautiful to learn in person.

The culture of a different tribe from mine.

The emotions that make tribes joyful are their cultures.

The vibrant colours, the elegant traditional dresses, the collection of different smells in a dish and the unique language a tribe communicating with each other.

My passion is to venture to all the different states from the north-east of India.

I would listen to the many stories they share, take part in their cultures, dances, traditions.

Devour many traditional cuisines.

And maybe find love.

Meeting someone from a different tribe has been on my mind.

Before that, I will venture, learn and grow together with different people.

"yǒu yuán qiān lǐ lái xiāng huì - A Chinese Proverb"

"Fate or destiny brings people together from a thousand miles away."

CHAPTER VIII

My love for dogs

Milo.

He's a stray dog in my small locality.
He ventures daily in search for food.
Like any nomad dog.

I feel elated to see many stray dogs wait patiently near the local meat vendors.
Even Milo likes to wait for meat thrown at him from them.

Day by day he sleeps there.

I soon met Miley after she curiously noticed me feeding Milo with leftover-bones.

Milo and I became close after my small generosity with him.
He likes to sit with me by the roadside.
I honestly like spending time with him.

a note:*Dogs are so precious. They are loyal. They are a blessing.*

and a passion for portrait arts

23

My passion as an artist stem back when I was young.

My parents sent me to art classes.
I was taught by Sir. Royalborne.
He taught us the basics of still art to more advance-level art.
He taught us shades and perspective.They are so important in a portrait sketch.
I knew I had a talent to draw anything with a pencil. But not portraits.

The first portraits I drew were during my college years. It was Frenkie De Jong and Eden Hazard.

It was 2020. I asked mum for money, to get a sketchbook.

I drew Tom Hanks, Robert Downey and Jennifer Lawrence.
Tom Hanks was my favourite.

Sketching for me takes me to a different place.

A calm place

Where I can connect with a feeling of solace and serenity.

CHAPTER X

Oh! and football

Cristiano Ronaldo.

Cristiano Ronaldo playing for Al'Nassr

My diary was filled with his newspaper articles every weekend when he plays.
He made me fall in love with football.
He's playing for Al'Nassr now. A Saudi League.
I never thought he would want to leave Madrid.

"..and then Ronaldooooo! WHAT A GOAL BY CRISTIANO RONALDO!!!"

"..SENSATIONAL!! THE GREATEST MARKSMAN IN THE HISTORY OF THE CHAMPIONS LEAGUE""..WITH AN ABSOLUTE

BEAUTY!"

Cristiano Roanldo's Champions League goal against La Vecchia Signora

He scored a dream of a goal against Juventus in the 2018 Champions League.

"*All the Juventus fans around us are on their feet - APPLAUDING!*"

He then played for the Italian giants the following season.
Real Madrid thanked him for all the years.
They never wanted him to stay. That was the hypocricy.
Ronaldo was in his early thirties. And Real Madrid wanted to build their squad around youth.

And they did.

Brazilian flairs.

Vinicius Jr. Young, athletic and agile.

Rodrygo, a boy from Sao Paulo.

Valverde, Camavinga, Arda Guler, Tchouameni.. under the leadership of Kroos and Modric.

Jude Bellingham with Zidane's no.5.

And soon Kyllian Mbappe.

Referred to as Los-Blancos, Los-Gallacticos, a team of Superstars, for the last few decades, now a team of elite, young and versatile gerneration, with the sounding leadership of past decade players.

Even Barcelona are looking forward towards their youthful generation of players in their locker-room.

Barcelona's 16 year-old, Lamine Yamal

The Premier League is one of the best leagues in football.

I've supported Chelsea FC for 10 years now. And for more years to come.

I love the club.

Right now, with the leadership of Mauricio Pochettino, I feel they have improved alot comparing to the previous season.

The one under Antonio Conte was absolutely breathtaking!

"A switch to a 3-4-3 formation, which hadn't often been seen in England, sparked a 13-game winning run that led to his side romping to the title." - GOAL.com

The one under Thomas Tuchel was also amazing!

It was late. Midnight.

Chelsea won the Champions League!

The adrenaline.

The passion.

Tuchel even brought out a white board on the field to break down tactics on one game.

The final was against Manchester City - the best team in

England for the last decade with Pep.

They couldn't break our defense.

We had the best defense in the league that season.

Chelsea FC winning the Champions League in 2021

Toni Rudiger -

"It makes me feel proud. This is something I couldn't imagine, but now it's finally true and I will

need some days to realise it. "

Kai Havertz with the winning goal.

The German had a lacklustre season, with no perfect position or role in the Chelsea formation, but he then played the false-9 role well. A role played by Messi.

Kai Havertz with a Champions League winner's medal

"I've waited 15 years for this moment and now it's here and it's so special. It's such an incredible feeling. Right now I want to thank my family, my parents, my siblings, my grandmother and my girlfriend. I don't know what to say, I'm so happy and now is the time for us all to celebrate."

Final Words

I begin by acknowledging that this book was a stepping stone in my journey as a writer.

Though it is only a short memoir shaped by the perspectives I held while growing up, the words across its chapters brought me a quiet sense of serenity — a return to the beguiled yet profound character I once was.

I will always find joy in placing my words onto the pages of a book. For it is there that I understand myself most clearly.

I will continue to write — not only to remember who I was, but to shape who I am yet to be.

The Reasons for Perpetuity is a second memoir encompassing a catalogue of the lovely moments I value; reflections on the fragments of time I wished could last forever, yet learned to cherish precisely because they could not.

available now on Amazon.

www.ingramcontent.com/pod-product-compliance
Lightning Source LLC
Chambersburg PA
CBHW051418130726
47989CB00007B/2981